THE YORKSHIRE CRICKET QUIZ BOOK

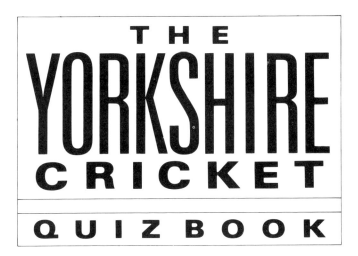

THE YORKSHIRE CRICKET QUIZ BOOK

TONY WOODHOUSE

MAINSTREAM
PUBLISHING

First published in Great Britain in 1989 by
MAINSTREAM PUBLISHING COMPANY (EDINBURGH) LTD
7 Albany Street, Edinburgh EH1 3UG

ISBN 1 85158 280 0 (paper)

British Library Cataloguing in Publication Data
 Woodhouse, Tony
 The Yorkshire cricket quiz book.
 1. Yorkshire. County cricket. Clubs:
 Yorkshire County Cricket Club, to 1983
 I. Title
 796.35′863′094281

ISBN 1-85158-280-0

Typeset in 11 on 13pt Imprint by Bookworm Typesetting, Edinburgh
Printed in Great Britain by Billings & Sons Ltd, Worcester

Contents

Acknowledgments

My grateful thanks to Mr C.F. Stansfield of Tong Park, Mr Marwood of Morley, and to Wombwell Cricket Lovers Society, for the loan of the photographs.

Thanks also for the valuable help of *Y. C. C. C. Year Books, Wisdens,* and the Association of Cricket Statisticians for material.

Especially too, John Featherston for his help in supplying photographs, correcting proofs and helping to collate the questions.

Introduction

To my knowledge this is the first quiz book to be produced solely in connection with the Yorkshire County Cricket Club.

My friends and colleagues, Tony Woodhouse and John Featherstone, have certainly been busy with numerous questions on Yorkshire cricket from all angles of the game, many of which will be new to many cricket followers. There are few aspects of Yorkshire cricket that have not been touched upon and it should prove fascinating to old and young alike.

W. Bryan Stott

(Bryan Stott was a member of the Yorkshire team from 1952-1963 and was a member of the championship winning sides of 1959, 1960, 1962 and 1963. He is now a prominent member of the Yorkshire C.C.C. Cricket Committee and an advanced coach.)

Questions

1 Who was the second Yorkshire player to captain England against South Africa?
2 Who was the first Yorkshire player to captain England against the West Indies?
3 Who was the second Yorkshire player to captain England against New Zealand?
4 Who was the first Yorkshire player to captain England against Pakistan?
5 Who was the first Yorkshire player to captain South Africa against Australia?
6 Who was the first Yorkshire player to captain England against Australia?
7 Who was the first Yorkshire player to score a century on his debut for England?
8 Who was the Yorkshire player to score the fastest Test Match fifty?
9 Who was the first Yorkshire player to take 200 Test wickets?
10 Who was the first Yorkshire player to take 100 Test wickets?

YORKSHIRE CAPTAINS

11 He was known as "Crackerjack".
12 The Malton Farmer.
13 Former Baildon skipper.
14 His father scored 112 centuries for Yorkshire.
15 His son played hockey for Yorkshire.
16 His father played centre-half for Bristol City.
17 His daughter married the Duke of Kent.
18 He came from Tiverton in Devonshire.
19 His brother was Rugby Union half-back for England.
20 The first post-war Bradford City footballer to play for Yorkshire.

SIR LEONARD HUTTON IN TEST CRICKET

21 When did he bat one-handed against the West Indies?

22 When did he carry his bat through the innings against Australia?

23 How many centuries did he score against Australia?

24 In which season did he score two centuries at Johannesburg?

25 How many centuries did he score against Pakistan?

26 How many double centuries did he score against the West Indies?

27 How many runs did he score in his first Test Match?

28 Who was his first Test partner in his first Test Match?

29 Who was his opening partner in his last Test Match?

30 Who bowled him out at Headingley for 0 in a Test Match?

UMPIRES PAST AND PRESENT

31 Batsman who challenged J.T. Tyldesley for middle-order England batting position.

32 Toured Australia in 1920-21 as understudy to Strudwick.

33 Batsman whose brother and father both played for Yorkshire too.

34 Almost a TV celebrity, he had never forsaken his native Barnsley.

35 Another who went to Leicester and a contemporary of the above.

36 Character from Bradford who, when asked by his senior whether the pitch would take spin at four o'clock, replied, "Nay, Wilfred, half-past".

37 He had a strange connection with Queen of the South.

38 Capped opener for Yorkshire who collected one century in first-class cricket.

39 World-famous umpire who collapsed on the field of play at Edgbaston.

40 Shoemaker and fast-bowler who was nicknamed "Shoey".

CONNECTIONS ABROAD

41 Which former Yorkshire all-rounder captained Tasmania v. M.C.C. in 1925 and made top score?

42 Which Yorkshire batsman and Huddersfield Town footballer played for Auckland?

43 Which Yorkshire cricketer played for Griqualand West before the Great War?

44 Which Yorkshire batsman captained South Africa?

45 Name the Yorkshire batsman who played for Tasmania with Jack Simmons.

CAPS AND EMBLEMS

46 What is the colour of the Yorkshire rose?

47 How many petals are there on the rose of a Yorkshire cap?

48 What are the Yorkshire colours?

49 Who introduced them to Yorkshire cricket?

50 Who were the last recipients of a Yorkshire cap?

DIFFICULT AUTHORS

Who was the author of each of the following books?

51 *Hints to Young Cricketers.*

52 *The Tempestuous Years.*

53 *English Cricket: What's Wrong & Why!*

54 *Wicket-Keeping.*

55 *Happy Go Johnny.*

UNUSUAL

56 Which famous cricketer was born at Scotch Springs?

57 Which famous cricketer was born at Summer Bridge?

58 Which famous cricketer died at Caserta?

11

59 Who scored 165 for Bedale v. Dalton in 1856 – and used to sleep with his bat?

60 A well-known coach who died during a cricket match at East Bierley while playing for his home club?

BRIAN CLOSE

61 What was the title of his autobiography that was written in 1978?

62 In which year did he play his last first-class match?

63 During which years was he captain of Yorkshire?

64 Which other county did he captain?

65 And for which years?

66 Who was the previous Yorkshire-born cricketer to captain Somerset?

67 How many times did Close captain England in Test Matches?

68 He was one of three England Captains from Yorkshire who were never beaten as Test Captains. Name the other two.

69 How many times did he lead Yorkshire to the County championship?

70 At the age of fourteen he was associated with which Football League club?

71 In which year was he first selected to tour Australia?

72 Which two other Football League clubs was he associated with?

73 How many centuries did he score for Yorkshire?

74 When he toured Australia in 1950-51, he took one wicket during the Test series. Whose?

75 Close was recalled to the England side in 1976 against the West Indies at Nottingham. Who was his only former Yorkshire team-mate in the same side?

W.E. BOWES

76 Where was he born?

77 Where did he spend his childhood life?

78 What does the "E" stand for?

79 With which Leeds club did he play as a youngster?
80 How many times did he take 100 wickets in a season for Yorkshire?
81 In 1932 he took his highest number of wickets in a season for Yorkshire. How many?
82 How many times did he play for England?
83 How many times did he dismiss Bradman?
84 How many wickets did he take for England?
85 How many runs did he score for England?
86 How many runs did he score in first-class cricket for Yorkshire?
87 How many wickets did he take for Yorkshire?
88 On what ground did he take 8 for 18 and 8 for 17 in the same match against Northants in 1935?
89 For which team did he play in first-class cricket before first playing for Yorkshire?
90 What was his best performance in Test cricket?
91 Against whom and when?
92 Which wicket-keeper took two catches off him in that innings?
93 Bowes also took 6 for 34 in a Test Match. When, where and against whom?
94 How were those wickets taken?
95 What was notable about that game?

PICTURE QUIZ – I

96 Who is in the centre of the middle row and who sits in front of him?

97 What are the names of this famous trio?

The "Vanity" Series

98   Who is this wicket-keeper?

99 Can you name this father of a famous captain?

100 In which year did this team win the championship?
101 Name the Sheffield United footballer second from the right in the top row.
102 And identify the future Glamorgan batsman on his left.

103 Who is this all-rounder?

104 And can you name this one?

105 Who was this Yorkshire Captain?

17

DAVID BAIRSTOW

106 Where was he awarded his County cap?

107 Where did he take his 1,000th victim for Yorkshire?

108 In 1970 he made his debut against Gloucestershire at Park Avenue. What was special about that occasion?

109 Against whom did he score his maiden century?

110 When and where?

111 During the 1978-79 tour of Australia, he flew out as a replacement for the injured wicket-keeper. Who was it he replaced?

112 In 1982 at Scarborough against Derbyshire, he equalled a world record. What was it?

113 Which two other wicket-keepers share that record?

114 Which Yorkshire record did Bairstow create in that match?

115 In the "Roses" match at Headingley in 1980, he made six catches in the innings, which beat a Yorkshire record. What was it?

R. ILLINGWORTH

116 Where was he born, and when?

117 When did he make his debut for Yorkshire?

118 Which other county did he play for?

119 When did he captain the latter county?

120 Who was the previous Leicestershire Captain to be a former Yorkshire player?

121 When was he awarded the C.B.E.?

122 When did he take nine for 42 against Worcestershire?

123 When did he lead England in Australia and regain the Ashes?

124 When did he play his last match for Yorkshire?

125 Which competition did Yorkshire win in 1983 under his captaincy?

1946 SEASON

126 Where did Yorkshire finish in the County Championship?

127 Who was the Captain?

128 Of the 1939 team, one player was killed in action and two retired. Name them.
129 Who was Yorkshire's left-arm slow bowler in his first full season?
130 Name the two batsmen who scored 1,000 runs for Yorkshire.
131 What was the total number of individual centuries scored during the season for Yorkshire?
132 In July, which county compiled 508 against Yorkshire?
133 Which Yorkshire players took part in the Test series against India?
134 Why did the match against Derbyshire at Chesterfield start twice?
135 Who was the only bowler to take over 100 wickets for Yorkshire in championship matches?

GENERAL

136 What relationship was there between C.E.M. Wilson and E.R. Wilson?
137 In which year did Wilfred Rhodes finish his Test Match career?
138 In a tenth-wicket stand of 149 for Yorkshire v. Warwickshire at Edgbaston in 1982, who beat the record held by Lord Hawke and David Hunter?
139 Who was better-known as "Old Ebor"?
140 What was his occupation?
141 What experiment took place at Headingley against Notts in May 1904?
142 What was David Denton's highest score for Yorkshire?
143 Who was known as "Jacker"?
144 In 1987 two new players joined the county. Name them.
145 In 1987 two players left the county before the season started. Name them.
146 What was the career-best score made by Richard Blakey against Gloucestershire at Headingley in 1987?
147 Where was the Fenner Trophy competition played annually?

148 In the fifth Test Match at Port of Spain between the West Indies and England in 1973-74, who made the individual scores of 99 and 112?

149 Which famous person in the history of cricket was born at Thirsk?

150 Who captained Cambridge University in 1938?

151 In 1948, who equalled the record of Percy Holmes, scoring a century in each innings of a "Roses" match?

152 Who was the first professional to be appointed captain of Yorkshire this century?

153 In 1948, two Yorkshire-born cricketers played a major part in the game at Taunton for Somerset against Yorkshire. Who were they?

154 At Wellingborough in 1949 against Northants, Yorkshire scored 523 runs of which one player scored over half. Who was that player?

155 When Yorkshire beat Gloucestershire by an innings and 76 runs at Harrogate in 1967, who took seven wickets in each innings?

156 In 1976, which two Yorkshire players were chosen to tour India and Sri Lanka?

157 What was strange about the pair obtained by Len Hutton for Yorkshire against Worcestershire in 1949?

158 Which three Yorkshire cricketers took part in the M.C.C. "A" team tour of Pakistan in 1955-56?

159 In 1967 at Hove against Sussex, who took nine wickets in one innings for the first time in his career?

160 Who scored his first century in any class of cricket against the Indians at Bradford in 1974?

161 In 1975, who scored 87 and took eight for 72 against Derbyshire at Scarborough?

162 Which former Yorkshire player was President of Scarborough Cricket Club in 1975?

163 Against the M.C.C. at Scarborough in 1951, which Yorkshire bowler obtained his 200th wicket of the season?

164 Which two former Yorkshire cricketers joined Leicestershire in 1960?

165 In 1978, why was there no cricket in the "Roses" match at Headingley on Spring Bank Holiday Monday?

166 This very fast bowler only played in two matches for Yorkshire, but he bowled out A.P.F. Chapman and Hubert Ashton at Fenners, as well as having Chapman caught out a second time for a duck. He became a schoolmaster at Denstone, Sedbergh and Barnard Castle, where he died in 1975 aged 75. Who was this cricketer?

167 This fast-bowler with a dubious action once bowled out the Australians at Scarborough in 1880, causing their first defeat of the tour. He came from Helmsley and was a cousin of a Yorkshire 2nd XI captain of the same name. Who was he?

168 This player captained Yorkshire in 1930 and shone at soccer with the Corinthians as well as being a good golfer, hockey player and fives player. He was a director of an indoor cricket school at Sunningdale from 1956 and died at Ludgrove School. Who was he?

169 Descended from a famous seafaring family, he lived at Wighill Park at one time and had been both a director of Leeds Cricket Football and Athletic Club as well as Sheffield United Cricket and Football Club. He shone at soccer and was President of the M.C.C. and of Yorkshire C.C.C. He played for Yorkshire for many years. Who was this gentleman?

170 This gentleman was another formidable fast-bowler who disguised the fact that he was actually born in Lancashire. He took five for 17 against Derbyshire in 1919. Who was he?

171 Who was the Scarborough batsman who made six consecutive centuries for them in 1938 and also represented Gentlemen v. Players, but was seldom able to play for his county?

172 A native of Heckmondwike, he played once for Yorkshire and later for Middlesex but is best known for being the father of a famous England Captain. Name, please.

173 This gentleman won the Grand National on Double Chance in 1925 and rode over 200 winners during his career. He played cricket for Yorkshire in 1911 and 1912. What was his name?

174 A rowing blue from Malton, he also played cricket for Oxford University, and was a good batsman and fast bowler for Yorkshire in the 1870s. A man of the cloth, he played for the Yorkshire Gentlemen from 1864 to 1900 and introduced Lord Hawke into the Yorkshire side. What is his name?

175 Took 11 for 155 for Cambridge v. Oxford University in 1875 and also was a soccer blue. A native of Codicote (Hertfordshire), he played for Yorkshire in 1875 and became vicar of Elsecar. What was his name?

MISCELLANEOUS - I

176 Which Yorkshire player played in the Grand Theatre Orchestra for 30 years?

177 Who was the youngest Yorkshire player to be awarded a benefit?

178 In which other sport did Peter J. Squires represent Yorkshire and England?

179 Who is the only player to have made over 2,000 runs and taken 200 wickets in a season?

180 Which Yorkshire player was involved in an unusual dismissal in a Test Match at The Oval?

181 Which Yorkshire player has been dismissed most times for a "pair" in Test Matches?

182 Name the Yorkshire player who assisted Derbyshire in John Player League matches only.

183 How many centuries did F.S. Jackson score for Yorkshire?

184 Which constituency did he represent as a Member of Parliament?

185 How many centuries did Len Hutton score on his tour of Australia in 1950- 51?

YORKSHIRE GROUNDS

What are the names of the cricket grounds where first-class cricket is or was played in the following places?

186 Harrogate

187 Scarborough (before their present ground)
188 Huddersfield
189 Halifax
190 Sheffield (up to 1973)
191 Scarborough (present ground)
192 Hull
193 Leeds
194 Bradford (from 1880)
195 Middlesbrough (present ground)

PICTURE QUIZ – 2

196 Can you name the future captain sitting on the extreme left of the front row?
197 Name the future captain sitting on his left.
198 Name the famous opening batsman standing second from the left, top row.
199 Second from the right in the top row stands a batsman said to be one of the most difficult players to dismiss during the period between the wars. Who was he?

200 Name this opening pair, at Scarborough in unfamiliar guise.

201 Here they are again. Where and when?

202 On which ground were these players taking part?
203 Who are the two players?

204 Two more Yorkshire stalwarts – who are they?
205 What caps are they wearing?

Whereabouts were the following cricketers born?

206 P.W. Jarvis
207 S.D. Fletcher
208 M.D. Moxon
209 A.A. Metcalfe
210 P. Carrick
211 R.J. Blakey
212 P.E. Robinson
213 J.D. Love
214 D.L. Bairstow
215 C. Shaw

FIRSTS

216 Which Yorkshire cricketer was the first to take a hat-trick of lbws in first-class cricket?
217 Who was the first Yorkshire player to score a century in his first Championship match?
218 Which Yorkshireman was the first to score 1,000 runs and take 100 wickets against Australia in Tests?
219 Who was the first modern professional Captain of England?
220 Who was the first English cricketer to perform a hat-trick in Test cricket?
221 Who was the first bowler to take 300 wickets in Test cricket?
222 Who was the first Yorkshire player to score a hundred during his Test debut at Lord's?
223 Who was the first England player to bat on each day in a five-day Test?
224 Which Yorkshire player took a wicket with his first ball in a Test Match?
225 Who was the first Yorkshire player to score a Test century?

What are the nicknames, noms-de-plume etc. of these Yorkshire players?

226 C.M. Old
227 D.L. Bairstow
228 Arthur Wood
229 Arthur Mitchell
230 N.W.D. Yardley
231 David Denton
232 Harold Bird
233 T.A. Jacques
234 George Ulyett
235 David Byas

DATES

236 In which season did Len Hutton first play for Yorkshire?
237 When did Yorkshire first win the County Championship under Lord Hawke?
238 When was the first Test Match won by England against Australia at Headingley?
239 When was the Yorkshire C.C.C. formed?
240 In which season did Percy Holmes last play for England?
241 In which season did Herbert Sutcliffe obtain his 100th hundred?
242 In which season did Chris Old obtain a century for Yorkshire v. Warwickshire in 37 minutes?
243 When did Frank Smailes take all ten wickets against Derbyshire?
244 When did Yorkshire dismiss Notts for 13 at Trent Bridge?
245 In which season did Don Wilson score 30 from an over off R.N.S. Hobbs?

246 Six grounds are now used in England for playing Test cricket, but a seventh has housed a Test Match in the past. Which ground?

247 Which Yorkshire fast-bowler became well-known as a sporting journalist with a Leeds newspaper?

248 Which Yorkshire Captain died in September 1971?

249 Which Yorkshireman was joint manager of the 1950-51 M.C.C. team to Australia?

250 Who succeeded Bobby Peel as Yorkshire's left-arm slow bowler?

251 At which ground was George Cawthray groundsman before coming to Headingley?

252 What was the connection between C.I. Thornton and Cecil Pepper?

253 Who scored two centuries for Yorkshire v. Notts at Sheffield in 1966?

254 Who averaged 60.73 for England in Test cricket?

255 Who succeeded Norman Yardley as Yorkshire captain?

256 Name the Yorkshire cricketer who in his debut season in 1919 scored 1,839 runs?

257 Who was the New Zealander who dismissed L. Hutton for nothing and one in his first Test Match?

258 When England regained the Ashes at The Oval in 1953, who made the top score of the match and how many did he score?

259 Who is the only Yorkshire bowler to have taken four wickets in four balls?

260 Which Yorkshire cricketer was killed in the Boer War?

BIRTHPLACES - 2

Which Yorkshire cricketers were born in the following places?

261 Eaglescliffe

262 Willingham Rectory

263 Nice
264 Farnborough (Hants)
265 Tavistock
266 Uppermill
267 Chelsea
268 Spofforth
269 Rochdale
270 Clitheroe

NICKNAMES - DIFFICULT

271 Joseph Rowbotham
272 Ephraim Lockwood
273 David Hunter
274 Wilf Barber
275 W.E. Bates
276 William Bates
277 C.E. Anson
278 P.W. Jarvis
279 A.G. Nicholson
280 J.T. Rawlin

MISCELLANEOUS - 3

281 Which Yorkshire batsman scored 315* for Yorkshire v. Middlesex at Lord's in 1925?
282 Who was the capped left-arm slow bowler for Yorkshire between Rhodes and Booth?
283 What was unusual about the Minor Counties Challenge match in 1933 in which Yorkshire took part?
284 Which county did they defeat?
285 What was the overall result?
286 What is the Yorkshire equivalent of the Hampshire Hogs?
287 After the 1950 season was over, which Yorkshire player resigned from the club and went into League cricket?
288 Which three cricketers have been members of as many as 12 championship-winning teams?

289 Which two Yorkshire cricketers opened against South Africa in 1955 in the Tests?

290 Bairstow, Balderstone, Close, Sidebottom, Taylor and Watson were Yorkshire players who appeared in the Football League after the last war. Who was the seventh?

291 Which Yorkshire cricketer had the name Pembroke as one of his forenames?

292 Which Yorkshire cricketer had the name Lancelot as one of his forenames?

293 Name the only amateur wicket-keeper to stump regularly for the Yorkshire C.C.C.

294 Which former Yorkshire cricketer had the name Vernon as one of his forenames?

295 Hampshire and Nicholson were two out of three cricketers capped by Yorkshire at the end of the 1963 season. Name the third.

PICTURE QUIZ – 3

296 Who is this record-breaking batsman?

297 On which ground was this photo taken?

298 Name this Yorkshire and England wicket-keeper.

299 Identify this Yorkshire Captain and future President.

300 Name these four Yorkshire players.

301 Who is presenting this trophy?

302 Who is this Yorkshire amateur?

303 Name this opening pair.
304 On which ground are they going out to bat?

305 Nostalgic memories abound from this famous ground. Where is it?

AFTER THE GREAT WAR – 1919 SEASON

306 Who was Yorkshire's Captain?

307 When did he first play for Yorkshire?

308 How many Championship matches did Yorkshire play?

309 What was Yorkshire's position in the table?

310 What were the duration and times of the Championship matches?

311 What were the conditions to determine the placings in the Championship table?

312 Who finished top of the Yorkshire batting averages?

313 Three players scored over 1,000 runs in Championship matches. Name them.

314 Who was top of the Yorkshire bowling averages in the Championship?

315 Only one Yorkshire player took over 100 Championship wickets for Yorkshire. Who was it and how many did he take?

RELATIONS

How are the following related?

316 Andrew and Luke Greenwood
317 Sir Len Hutton and Simon Dennis
318 Herbert and W.H.H. Sutcliffe
319 E.T. and E.W. Hirst
320 Norman Kilner and Irving Washington
321 A. and A.B. Sellers
322 J. and J.H. Hampshire
323 D. and J. Denton
324 John Thewlis and E. Lockwood
325 G.G. Macaulay and J. Lister

JOHN PLAYER SPECIAL LEAGUE

326 Name the nine home venues used by Yorkshire.
327 What is the lowest number of runs scored in an innings against Yorkshire?
328 Which Yorkshire player has taken a hat-trick in the competition?
329 What is the best bowling performance in the competition by a Yorkshire player?
330 Who was the first player to take 100 wickets for Yorkshire?

BOWLERS

Describe the type of bowling favoured by these bowlers.

331 Wilfred Rhodes
332 Abe Waddington
333 G. Freeman
334 Bobby Peel
335 Mike Cowan
336 R. Appleyard
337 E. Leadbeater

338 J. Birkenshaw
339 G.A. Cope
340 M.W. Booth

BATSMEN

Which is the left-handed batsman amongst the following?

341 Halliday, Hutton, Leyland, Mitchell
342 B.B. Wilson, J.T. Brown senior, Vic Wilson, Yardley
343 Oldroyd, Haigh, W.H. Wilkinson, W. Barber
344 Washington, Denton, Tunnicliffe, Rhodes
345 Padgett, Taylor, Stott, Illingworth
346 Halliday, Boycott, Phil Sharpe, Kevin Sharp
347 Lowson, Watson, Denton, Hampshire
348 Binks, Bowes, Birkenshaw, Brennan
349 Holmes, Sutcliffe, Hirst, Blakey
350 Hamer, Harbord, Hatton, Hayley

TEST MATCHES – 2

351 What age was E.R. Wilson when he made his Test debut v. Australia at Sydney in 1921?
352 What was the lowest team score to be made at Headingley?
353 When was the first Test Match played at Headingley?
354 What was the highest innings in Test cricket scored at Headingley by one side?
355 In 1902 Wilfred Rhodes took seven for 17 in an innings against Australia. Where?
356 In the 1952 Test against India at Headingley, F.S. Trueman took three wickets in eight balls. Who were his three victims?
357 Which Yorkshire player made his debut for England in the above match?
358 Who was the second Yorkshireman to score 1,000 runs and take 100 wickets in Test cricket?

359 In the first Test Match at Kingston, Jamaica in 1954, which two Yorkshire batsmen opened the innings for England against the West Indies?

360 Which one of them scored a century in that game?

361 When the Australians played England in the third Test Match at Headingley in 1961, this match was afterwards referred to as "Trueman's Match". Why?

COUNTY CHAMPIONSHIP

362 When were Yorkshire champions for the first time?

363 In which years were they joint champions?

364 Who were they joint champions with in those seasons?

365 What is the lowest Yorkshire have ever finished in the Championship?

366 In what year was that?

367 How many times have Yorkshire been declared County champions?

368 How many Championships did Yorkshire win between the wars?

369 When did Yorkshire last win the County Championship?

370 In two seasons Yorkshire went through the season unbeaten without winning the County Championship. Name them.

371 Since winning their first officially recognised Championship in 1893, Yorkshire won more matches than they lost in every season until when?

WILFRED RHODES – I

372 Which Scottish club did he join at the age of 18?

373 When and where was his first Test Match?

374 Which famous Test cricketer was playing his last Test at the same time?

375 Where was he born?

376 When did he first play for Yorkshire and against whom?

377 Where was he born?
378 When was he President of Yorkshire C.C.C.?
379 In which year was he President of the M.C.C.?
380 At school at Harrow, which famous person was his fag?
381 When he captained England in 1905 when England were unbeaten, what was remarkable about his performances?

CHAMPIONSHIP WINNERS

In which championship-winning sides did the following players represent Yorkshire?

382 S. Allen, L. Ryder, G. Wilson
383 G. Boycott, K. Taylor, J.D. Woodford
384 H. Hayley, G. Ulyett, T. Wardall
385 J. Brumfitt, A. Hamer, H. Sutcliffe
386 J.T. Bell, M. Leyland, G.G. Macaulay
387 H. Beaumont, W.E. Bowes, W. Watson
388 H.D. Bird, R.K. Platt, J.V. Wilson
389 R. Kilner, G.W.A. Render, A.C. Williams
390 W.E. Bates, A.W. Lupton, B.B. Wilson
391 W. Barber, J.H. Pearson, H. Verity

392 Top row, second from left. Who is this Yorkshire cricketer connected with Notts and Nottingham Forest?

393 Top row, third from left. Name this famous slow-bowler for Yorkshire and England.

394 Top row, third from right. Identify this Yorkshire fast bowler.

395 Top row, second from right. Name Yorkshire's fast scorer in more ways than one.

396 Bottom row, far left. Who is this Yorkshire and Leicestershire left-hander?

397 Bottom row, second from left. Name this Yorkshire and England wicket-keeper.

398 Bottom row, second from right. Identify this Yorkshire stalwart of the Yardley era.

399 This is an aerial view of which ground?

400   Who is this cheerful Yorkshire left-arm slow bowler?

401 Who are this pair of Yorkshire batsmen?

AUSTRALIAN TESTS

402 Who scored 144* for England after England had lost three wickets for 57?

403 The next highest scorer in the same innings was also a Yorkshire player. Who?

404 Who averaged 190 for England in the 1928-29 series?

405 Who averaged 87.20 for England in 1930 and also made the highest aggregate?

406 On the 1936-37 tour, who opened batting with C.J. Barnett at Adelaide?

407 In the 1903-04 Tests, who bowled most overs, most maidens and took most wickets for England?

408 Who took the first wicket ever to fall in Test cricket?

409 Who took the first catch ever in Test cricket?

410 Who was the first fielder to take three catches in one Test Match?

411 Two Yorkshire-born wicket-keepers kept wicket at Melbourne in 1921. Name them.

412 Name the seven Yorkshire cricketers from whom the England sides would have been chosen against Australia in 1938.

413 In 1938 Bradford and Leeds each had three committee members serving its interests. How many had Sheffield?

414 In the drawn game at Huddersfield against Hampshire, which bowler took eight for 63 for Yorkshire?

415 When Surrey were bowled out for 52 and 162 at Sheffield, Bowes took six for 32 in the first innings and a spinner took five for 45 in the second. Name him.

416 Which famous former President of Yorkshire C.C.C. died in 1938?

417 After 17 games in the championship, Yorkshire had won eleven, rain had interfered with the six draws and only Gloucestershire had headed them on the first innings. In the next match at Lord's, Yorkshire were beaten by eight wickets. What was significant about the defeat?

418 At The Oval, Yorkshire suffered their second defeat without Hutton, Leyland, Verity and Bowes. Who scored 77 and 174* for Surrey?

419 In the matches against the two Universities, Yorkshire-born players made top score for each University against Yorkshire. Name them.

420 Who was the former Yorkshire player who made top score in Scotland's second innings v. Yorkshire at Harrogate?

421 Name the four Yorkshire bowlers to take 100 wickets in the season.

A WET SEASON - 1958

422 Yorkshire were 24 for six against Lancashire at Headingley. Who did the damage for Lancashire?

423 Another collapse for Yorkshire against Northants. All out 67 and 65. Who was responsible?

424 A Middlesex leg-spinner rattled Yorkshire out for 101 at Headingley by taking six for 40. Who was he?

425 This batsman at The Oval scored 155 against Yorkshire when no other player in the match could reach 50. Who was he?

426 In the same game a Surrey bowler took six for 18 and five for 48. Who was he?

427 The spinners had a field day against Essex at Middlesbrough. One of ours made 81* and then took seven for 49 in Essex's first innings. Who was he?

428 A Yorkshire fast bowler helped to bowl Oxford University out for 75 at The Parks by taking five for 19. Name him.

429 During the Test v. New Zealand at Manchester, which England won by an innings and 13 runs, a Yorkshire batsman opened the innings and scored 66. Who was he?

430 Hampshire collapsed from 82 for 0 to 118 all out thanks to two bowlers who took five for 23 and five for 45. Who were the two bowlers?

431 Yorkshire won the Minor Counties Championship by beating Oxfordshire at Bridlington. Who made 143 for Yorkshire?

SCHOFIELD HAIGH

432 How many wickets did he take for Yorkshire?

433 What was his best bowling performance?

434 How many centuries did he score for Yorkshire?

435 Where was he born?

436 What appointment did he undertake when he left Yorkshire C.C.C.?

437 How many times did he perform the hat-trick for Yorkshire?

438 How many runs did he score for Yorkshire?

439 Which year did he first play for Yorkshire?

440 Where did he tour abroad with the M.C.C.?

441 Who was his captain on that tour?

442 When did he first go on an England tour abroad?
443 Who was the Captain?
444 How many Test runs did he score altogether?
445 How many runs did he score for Yorkshire?
446 How many wickets did he take for Yorkshire?
447 Which was his last year in first-class cricket?
448 How many times did he take 100 wickets or more in a season?
449 What was his highest score in first-class cricket?
450 How many times did he score 1,000 runs in a season in England?
451 Who was his last victim in Test cricket?
452 When and where did he play his last Test Match?
453 1930 was Rhodes' last season as well as Bradman's first time in England. How many times did they face one another?
454 How many times did Rhodes take Bradman's wicket?
455 Who was Rhodes' first victim in first-class cricket?
456 In matches where Yorkshire took the field, in how many matches did Rhodes fail to take a wicket during his first season?

457 In the match with Kent at Harrogate in 1904, the match was abandoned on the second day. Why?
458 Who has carried his bat through an innings on the most occasions for Yorkshire?
459 How many times did he carry his bat through an innings?
460 Which touring team did Yorkshire defeat at Huddersfield in 1878?
461 A touring team played at Harrogate in 1901. Which team was it?
462 When the Australians played at Bradford in 1905, one Yorkshire bowler had the following bowling analysis: – 9-76-. What was his name?

463 Who scored a double century for Yorkshire against Scotland at Scarborough in 1951?

464 In 1909, Yorkshire met the Australians twice, drawing both games. They were also involved in two other games against the tourists. What was unusual about those games?

465 Where were those games played?

466 In 1952, against which county did J.V. Wilson score 230?

467 In 1974, who made the highest individual score for Yorkshire in the County Championship?

468 Which team beat Yorkshire in two days for the first time in their history in 1965? Where did they play?

469 Name the three amateur Yorkshire wicket-keepers who have played for England.

470 In 1953, who hit his highest individual score of 259* for Yorkshire against Worcestershire?

471 Which Yorkshire cricketer performed the double in 1964?

1980 SEASON

472 Who received their County caps during 1980?

473 In scoring his ninth century against Lancashire at Old Trafford, whose "Roses" record did Geoff Boycott equal?

474 Who resigned the captaincy after two seasons?

475 How many dismissals did David Bairstow make in first-class cricket?

476 Which two cricketers had a joint benefit?

477 These young Yorkshire players were celebrating a Championship win in 1959. Name the player on the far left.

478 Who stands second from the left? . . .

479 . . . and third from the left?

480 Who is fourth from the right? . . .

481 . . . and second from the right?

482 Name the player on the far right of the photo.

483 Celebrating that same Championship win, name the player
on the far left.

484 Who stands in the front row on the left?

485 Name the player in the centre of the photo.

486 Who is situated on the far right of the picture?

487 Which Yorkshire cricketer joined the first-class umpires list?

488 Who made the highest score of 161 for Yorkshire in the County Championship?

489 Who was the Yorkshire Captain?

490 Which former Yorkshire Captain died on 22 February aged 73?

491 How many sixes did David Bairstow hit in his 103* against Derbyshire at Derby?

492 When Martyn Moxon scored 111 against Derbyshire at Sheffield, what feat had he performed?

493 Which Yorkshireman dismissed G. Boycott with his first ball in County cricket?

494 Who captained Yorkshire against Warwickshire at Scarborough in the absence of Old and Boycott?

495 Two players scored centuries at Abbeydale Park for Derbyshire against Yorkshire. One was Alan Hill. Who was the other?

496 Which fast bowler played his first game for Yorkshire against Sussex at the age of 16?

CRICKET AUTHORS

Name the authors of these books by Yorkshire cricketers.

497 *Cricket Campaigns*
498 *Just My Story*
499 *Double International*
500 *Put to the Test*
501 *50 Years in Cricket*
502 *Family Argument*
503 *That's Out*
504 *Recollections and Reminiscences*
505 *Cricket Triumphs and Troubles*
506 *Cricket for Schoolboys*

PUBLIC SCHOOLS

With which school do you associate the following?

507 N.W.D. Yardley
508 E.R. Wilson
509 W. Rhodes
510 A.T. Barber
511 D.V. Brennan
512 A.B. Sellers
513 W.G. Keighley
514 Hon. F.S. Jackson
515 Sir William Worsley
516 G.H. Hirst

ASSOCIATIONS

Which cricketer do you associate with the following?

517 J.T. Brown senior
518 Hirst
519 Percy Holmes
520 Tom Emmett
521 Louis Hall
522 W. Slinn
523 M.W. Booth
524 W.B. Stott
525 Kirkheaton
526 Fulneck

NUMBERS

With which Yorkshire cricketers do you associate the following?

527 307
528 341?
529 4,187
530 364

531 1,294
532 10 for 10
533 555
534 3,429
535 50,138
536 554
537 151
538 2,385; 208
539 102.53
540 17 for 91
541 6 for 70, 5 for 45; 111 and 117*

CUP COMPETITIONS

Which League competitions do you associate with the following cups and trophies?

542 The Priestley Cup
543 The Waddilove Cup
544 The Sykes Cup
545 The Hepworth Cup
546 The Kerridge Cup
547 The Jack Hampshire Trophy
548 The Hepworth Trophy
549 The Collinson Cup
550 The Billy Oates Memorial Trophy
551 The Hare Cup

MISCELLANEOUS – 5

552 Which Yorkshire batsman led Transvaal to a Currie Cup win in 1903?
553 Who is David Ryder?
554 Which was Percy Holmes' last season in first-class cricket for Yorkshire?
555 When did Geoffrey Boycott score his first Test century?
556 Who was it against and where?

557 Name the Yorkshire amateur who took a team to South Africa in 1927-28.

558 Ken Davidson played for Yorkshire as both an amateur and a professional. At which other sport was he a professional?

559 Who is generally recognised as having the largest-ever benefit up to the Second World War?

560 Who scored the most runs for England in 1970 in the series against the Rest of the World?

561 Which Yorkshire-born player topped the Cambridge University batting and bowling averages in 1973?

562 Which Yorkshire wicket-keeper has taken the most victims in a season?

563 What was that total of victims?

564 Contained in that total was a record for a wicket-keeper. What was the record?

565 Who was known as "Clear Gum"?

566 Which Yorkshire-born Poet Laureate wrote a poem with cricket as its theme?

1988 SEASON

567 How many Yorkshire cricketers completed their 1,000 runs in first-class cricket?

568 Moxon and Metcalfe were two of them. Who was the third?

569 Who took the most wickets for Yorkshire?

570 Who were the two Yorkshire players dismissed for 98 against Somerset?

571 Who scored 216* for Yorkshire?

572 Yorkshire completed the season with a win at Trent Bridge. Who produced one of the finest all-round performances for Notts in that game?

573 Who bowled most overs for Yorkshire?

574 Which fielder took most catches for Yorkshire?

575 Who won the Bradford League Championship?

576 Which club does David Byas captain when not in the Yorkshire side?

577 Name the cricket club which had the assistance of the Australian Test players, Dean Jones and Tony Dodemaide, during 1988.

578 Which club does Steve Oldham captain?

579 What position did Yorkshire finish in the Refuge Assurance League?

580 Who has just written a biography of a famous Yorkshire cricketer?

581 Who is the cricketer?

582 Name the two Yorkshire-born wicket-keepers who headed the wicket-keeping figures.

583 Name the Yorkshireman who headed the Gloucestershire batting averages.

584 Which Yorkshireman finished second in the Northamptonshire bowling averages?

585 Name the Yorkshireman who appeared for Notts.

586 Name the Yorkshireman who headed the Somerset bowling averages.

PICTURE QUIZ - 6

587 Close takes a brilliant catch to dismiss Dawkes in 1955. Name the wicket-keeper and the other fielder.

588 Fred Trueman during *This is Your Life*. Who is the
Yorkshire cricketer on his left?

589 Yorkshire 2nd XI champions of 1984, captained by Colin
Johnson with Richard Lumb on his left. Name the other
cricketers on the front row.
590 Who is the coach standing on the right?

591 Who are this pair of Yorkshire cricketers?

592 Jack Sokell of Wombwell Cricket Lovers presents a cheque to whom?

593 A Yorkshire Schools Under-15 side. Who is sitting in the centre of this picture?

594 Who is the youngster on his right-hand side?

595 This Yorkshire 2nd XI picture was taken in the early 1920s. Who is the cricketer sitting down on the right?

596 Ernest Holdsworth, the Captain, is in the middle. Who is behind him in the sports jacket?

A MIXED BAG

597 At Hove in 1949, who scored a century in each innings against Sussex?

598 In 1952, in the third Test at Old Trafford, two Yorkshiremen made an important contribution. Name the two players involved.

599 What were their contributions?

600 Who took three wickets in four balls against Surrey at Sheffield in 1956?

601 Which two Yorkshire players took part in a last-wicket stand of 37 against Worcestershire at Worcester, which resulted in a one-wicket win for Yorkshire?

602 What made Don Wilson's contribution especially notable?

603 When Yorkshire were dismissed for 23 by Hampshire at Middlesbrough in 1965, what was their previous record low score?

604 Against whom and when did they make this score?

605 Who took seven for 37 at Colchester in 1970 against Essex?

606 With bowling figures of six for 14 at Worcester against Worcestershire in the John Player League in 1975, which player had his best bowling analysis in any competition?

607 Who was awarded a Testimonial by Yorkshire in 1984?

608 In 1949, which player scored a double century in the "Roses" match to equal the record of M. Leyland and R.H. Spooner?

609 In 1953, who bowled 76 overs in an innings for Yorkshire against Worcestershire at Worcester?

610 In 1956, who performed the hat-trick against Gloucestershire at Sheffield?

611 Who took 14 for 196 in 1956 for the M.C.C. against the Orange Free State at Bloemfontein?

SCHOOLS – PRESENT-DAY ASSOCIATIONS

With which schools do you associate the following?

612 W.H.H. Sutcliffe

613 S.P. Coverdale

614 P.B. Brayshay

615 R.A. Hutton

616 M.G. Crawford

617 P.A. Gibb

618 J.P. Whiteley

619 J. Lister

620 A. Dalton

621 P.J. Kippax

SCHOOLS – PAST ASSOCIATIONS

622 Sir Archibald White

623 G.G. Macaulay

624 W.E. Harbord
625 Frank Mitchell
626 C.E.M. Wilson

E. WAINWRIGHT

627 When did he first play for Yorkshire?
628 Against whom did he score his maiden century?
629 What type of bowler was he?
630 Where was he born?
631 What was his highest score in first-class cricket?
632 When did he make his Test debut?
633 How many Tests did he play?
634 How many times did he perform the "double" in first-class cricket?
635 Which club did he join after leaving Yorkshire?
636 Which famous cricket writer was his assistant coach at Shrewsbury College?

FOOTBALL CLUBS – I

637 This former cricket ground was where Edmund Peate once took eight for five v. Surrey, and was close to a famous football ground. Where was this cricket ground?
638 Who play on the famous football ground?
639 A Rugby League club still plays on this ground next to a cricket field which is now dormant, and was not long since used for County cricket and League cricket. What was its name?
640 This thriving Rugby League club plays next to a cricket ground with a stand shared by both separating them. The cricket ground is still used for Test and county cricket but not by the local League club, which has disbanded. Where is it?
641 Which former Football League club played next to a former county cricket ground?

642 Which former Yorkshire cricket ground opened in 1855 has now had a football stand built on it, whilst the old cricket pavilion has been pulled down and replaced by part of the stand?

643 On which present-day Football League ground did Yorkshire play Kent in 1890?

644 This cricket ground is still used for an occasional Sunday League match and is also used by a Rugby Union club. Before the war it belonged to the local Football League side, which has since been rehoused. Where is it?

645 This Rugby Union club plays on part of a large field shared by the cricket ground. Where is it?

646 The oldest soccer club in the world played alongside this ground, which is also used by the local Rugby Union club. Where is it?

YORKSHIRE EXILES – I

Which County did the following players assist after they left Yorkshire?

647 F. Jakeman

648 G.A. Smithson

649 C.C. Clifford

650 J.P. Whitehead

651 N. Kilner

652 J.M. Cownley

653 W.E. Bates

654 N.F. Horner

655 J.T. Bell

656 J.R. Ashman

EXILES WITH TWO COUNTIES

Which two Counties did the following play for when they left Yorkshire?

657 J. Birkenshaw

658 B. Wood

659 J.B. Bolus

660 Which two minor Counties did P.J. Kippax play for?

PICTURE QUIZ – 7

661 Who is the batsman on the right?

662 This cricket pavilion is on a League ground famous as the place where George Hirst and Wilfred Rhodes learnt their cricket. Where is it?

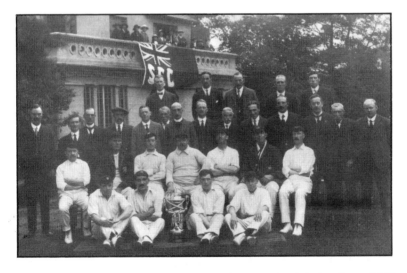

663 Sydney Barnes is seated second from the left in the middle row. Where is this?

664 A familiar figure. Who is he?

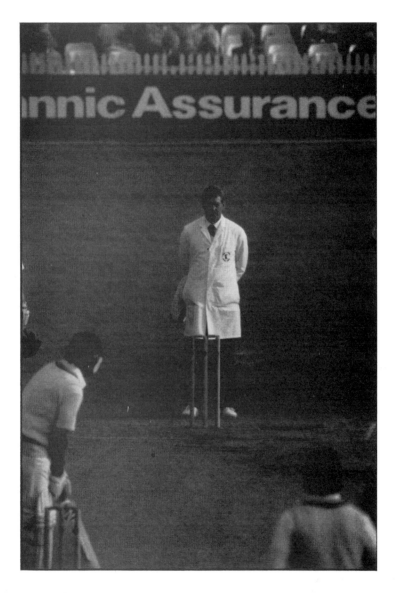

665 Another umpire, although perhaps not quite as familiar.
Who is he?

666 A monument to Hirst and Rhodes. Where is it?

667 Two great cricketers of the past, at Headingley. Name them.

668 Unusual view of a famous ground. Where is it?

669 Who is this former Yorkshire skipper?
670 At which ground and match was this photo taken?

FOOTBALL CLUBS - 2

Which senior football clubs did the following Yorkshire cricketers play for?

671 A. Sidebottom
672 A. Ramage
673 C. Balderstone
674 A. Waddington
675 D.B. Close
676 K. Taylor
677 T.J.D. Birtles
678 D.L. Bairstow
679 W. Watson
680 Alonzo Drake
681 W.H. Wilkinson
682 G. Waller
683 F.H. Sugg
684 W.E. Bates
685 W.H. Micklethwait
686 A. Hamer

MISCELLANEOUS - 6

687 Which bespectacled, balding opening batsman moved from Yorkshire to Essex?
688 Which two bowlers were released by the County after the 1980 season?
689 Which Yorkshire cricketer scored a century on his debut in first-class cricket, but not in a Yorkshire match?
690 Which team was he playing for?
691 Who was known as "Long John of Pudsey"?
692 Which was the last County to win the Championship in three consecutive seasons?
693 In which years did they last perform that feat?
694 Which County did Bob Platt join after leaving Yorkshire?
695 Yorkshire played a tie in 1954. Who was it against and where?

696 In 1966, name the four Yorkshire bowlers who captured 100 first-class wickets during the season.

697 Which cricket ground in Yorkshire do you associate with the names C.I. Thornton and T.N. Pearce?

698 Who was the first batsman to score 2,000 runs or more in a season for Yorkshire?

699 Who scored 260* for Yorkshire v. Essex at Colchester in 1970?

700 In 1946, this Yorkshire batsman scored 61 in a Test trial: more than he had obtained in any innings for Yorkshire. Who was he?

701 Which Glamorgan player scored a century in each innings against Yorkshire at Middlesbrough in 1976?

702 What did H.D. Read and M. Nichols do in 1935?

703 In which year was the electronic scoreboard installed at Headingley?

704 Name the three Yorkshire players who toured India, Pakistan and Ceylon in 1951-52.

705 What was significant about the Duke and Duchess of Kent's visit to the Kent v. Yorkshire match at Canterbury on 1 August 1968?

706 Name the two former Yorkshire players who received their County caps for Derbyshire in 1980.

707 Name the former Yorkshire player to obtain his County cap for Notts in 1980.

708 Who was secretary of Leicestershire before becoming secretary of Yorkshire?

709 Which former Yorkshire batsman topped the Oxfordshire batting averages in 1980?

710 Whom did D.B. Close succeed as the Yorkshire captain?

711 Whose grandson managed Southampton Football Club?

712 Who succeeded Sir William Worsley as President of Yorkshire C.C.C.?

713 What have or had the following gentlemen in common. Padley, Nash and Lister?

714 Who scored his maiden century for Yorkshire in the Championship match against Somerset at Sheffield in 1973?

715 Which Yorkshire batsman played Rugby Union for Driffield?

716 Which current England Rugby Union player has played for the Yorkshire 2nd XI?

1948

717 Who was the Yorkshire Captain?

718 Who was the Yorkshire beneficiary?

719 What position did Yorkshire occupy in the Championship table?

720 Who were the four players who scored over 1,000 runs for Yorkshire?

721 Who did Yorkshire lose their first two matches to in 1948?

722 Who was the Yorkshire player who scored two centuries in one match against Lancashire at Old Trafford?

723 Name the five Australians who recorded centuries in first-class matches in Yorkshire.

724 Who was the New Zealander who scored 208* for the M.C.C. v. Yorkshire at Scarborough?

725 When Derbyshire bowled out Yorkshire for 44 and were grovelling at 37 for six in their second innings, who had taken 10 for 25 in 31 overs and one ball at that time?

726 At Leeds against Yorkshire, Cyril Washbrook scored a fine 170 but one other Lancashire batsman also reached three figures. He belonged to a famous cricketing family. Name him.

GEORGE HERBERT HIRST

727 What was his highest individual score in first-class cricket?

728 How many times did he perform the cricketer's "double" of 1,000 runs and 100 wickets in a season?

729 How many centuries did he score for Yorkshire?

730 In which year did he receive a benefit with Yorkshire?

731 How much did his record benefit raise for him?

732 This total was not beaten until 1925. Who was the cricketer who beat his financial total?
733 What type of bowler was he?
734 Where did he score his first century?
735 In which season did he first tour abroad?
736 What was his bowling average in the Test Matches on that tour?

YORKSHIRE EXILES – 2

Which county did the following play for after they left Yorkshire?

737 R. Illingworth
738 R. Booth
739 C.W.J. Athey
740 E. Leadbeater
741 S.J. Rhodes
742 C. Lee
743 K. Gillhouley
744 B. Stead
745 M.K. Bore
746 E.P. Robinson

1988

747 Who is Chairman of the Yorkshire C.C.C. Cricket Sub-Committee?
748 Who is Chairman of the Yorkshire C.C.C. Committee?
749 Who is Secretary of the Yorkshire C.C.C.?
750 Who is Treasurer of the Yorkshire C.C.C.?
751 Who is President of the Yorkshire C.C.C.?
752 Who is Editor of the *White Rose* magazine?
753 Who is Captain of the Yorkshire 2nd XI?
754 Who is cricket correspondent of *The Yorkshire Post*?
755 Who is cricket correspondent of *The Telegraph and Argus*?
756 Who is cricket correspondent of *The Yorkshire Evening Post*?

757 Who is cricket correspondent of *The Hull Daily Mail*?
758 Who are the owners of Headingley cricket ground?
759 Who owns the Abbeydale Park cricket ground?
760 Who is the Patroness of the Yorkshire C.C.C.?
761 Which Yorkshire wicket-keeper during his career is now just eight victims in front of David Bairstow in his aggregate of dismissals?

PICTURE QUIZ – 8

762 Who is this present-day Yorkshire cricketer?

763 Two other former Yorkshire cricketers – can you name them?

764 Where was this taken and what is their significance?

765 Where was this picture taken?
766 Who is the lonely fielder?

767 Going out to bat. Who is this?

768 Identify this venue.

769 Carrick gives out Yorkshire caps at Scarborough to Peter Hartley and another player. Whom?

770 Name the player on the left.
771 The other cricketer became groundsman at Headingley.
Name him.

UMPIRES – 2

772 Name the five umpires on the 1988 list who had played for Yorkshire?

773 Which former umpire made his debut for Yorkshire as a fast bowler in 1946?

774 Which Yorkshire umpire won the Gillette Man of the Match Award in the 1969 final?

775 Which former Gloucestershire wicket-keeper came from Yorkshire?

776 This old umpire from Batley was a leading opening batsman for Yorkshire.

TEST MATCHES – 3

777 Which Yorkshireman topped the England bowling averages during the 1954-55 tour of Australia?

778 Which Yorkshireman topped the England bowling averages during the 1946-47 tour of Australia?

779 Who was the only Yorkshireman to perform a hat-trick in Test cricket?

780 Who was the first Yorkshireman to score fifty or more in a Test Match?

781 Who was the first English cricketer to perform the double of 1,000 runs and 100 wickets in Test Match cricket?

PROBLEMS

782 Who took five for 8 in his first match for Yorkshire?

783 What performance did he achieve in the second innings of the match?

784 Name the Yorkshire players who were chosen for the M.C.C. tour of India in 1939-40.

785 If N.E.J. Pocock was the sixth since the war for Hampshire, who was Yorkshire's sixth?

786 Which Yorkshire opening bowler since the war played centre-half for York City?

787 Who was the first batsman to score 2,000 runs in one season for Yorkshire?

788 Which former opening bowler was appointed scout to the Warwickshire C.C.C. during the year 1970?

789 Which spinner took most wickets for Yorkshire in the County Championship in 1972?

790 Who was Vivienne Lance?

791 With which cricket ground in Yorkshire would you associate the name Jack Douglas as groundsman?

G. BOYCOTT

792 Where did he play his 100th Test Match?

793 In which first-class seasons did he average over 100?

794 In which year was he appointed Yorkshire Captain?

795 In how many Tests did he captain England?

796 How many first-class runs did he score during his career?

797 What was his average?

798 Against whom did he score a century in each innings for Yorkshire?

799 On what date did he score his 100th century?

800 Who was his partner at the time?

801 Who was the innings against?

802 Who was bowling to him when he completed this feat?

803 How many other players had scored a hundred centuries?

804 Against whom and when did he average 4.33 in a Test series?

805 How many runs did he score in first-class cricket for Yorkshire in 1971? . . .

806 . . . And what was his average?

807 How many centuries did he score for Yorkshire?

808 How many Test hundreds did he score?

809 Which district does he represent on the Yorkshire Committee?

810 How many Championship-winning teams was he a member of?

811 On what date was he capped by Yorkshire?

812 How was Boycott dismissed in his last innings for Yorkshire?

813 How many Test Matches did he play in?

814 Who was his 300th Test victim?

815 Who took the catch?

816 Who was his first Test Captain?

817 Who were his first opponents in first-class cricket?

818 What was the date of the match?

819 Who was the Yorkshire Captain at the time?

820 Which two other Yorkshire players made their debuts in the same match?

821 Against which County did he perform the hat-trick three times?

822 Against which other team did he perform the hat-trick?

823 In 1954 v. Kent at Dover, he took eight for 28. What was special about this feat?

824 He obtained two of his three centuries in first-class cricket for Yorkshire. Who was his other century for and against?

825 Who was the first victim whom he bowled out in a first-class match?

826 Who was his first victim in Test cricket?

827 When serving on the Yorkshire Committee, which district did he represent?

828 In which season did he take 14 for 123 at The Oval v. Surrey?

829 On which ground did he take seven for 15 against Glamorgan?

830 Against which touring team did he take five for 19 at Bradford?

831 Only one Yorkshire bowler performed more hat-tricks in first-class cricket. Name him.

832 In Test Matches he took 64 catches in all. How many Yorkshire cricketers took more?

MISCELLANEOUS – 7

833 At Worksop against Nottinghamshire in 1966, this bowler performed the second hat-trick of his career. Who was it?

834 Which Yorkshire cricketer made his debut for the County on 1 August 1979?

835 What type of bowler was Arthur Booth?

836 What distinction did he have in his only season of regular first-class cricket?

837 Who was sacked by Arsenal and sacked by Yorkshire?

838 Who was known as "Lonza"?

839 Who was "Bobby from Churwell"?

840 Who performed the hat-trick in 1973 for Surrey at Headingley?

841 In 1980, when David Bairstow scored 145 for Yorkshire against Middlesex at Scarborough, it became the highest-ever score by a Yorkshire wicket-keeper. What was the previous best and by whom?

842 In 1974, which two players ran six for Surrey in a Sunday League against Yorkshire at The Oval?

843 Who was the Yorkshire wicket-keeper between Binks and Bairstow?

844 Who scored his first century for Yorkshire in 1980 on the day after he had been chosen in the 12 for the fifth Test at Headingley against the West Indies?

845 Where did Len Hutton score his 100th century and when was it?

846 In 1976, which two former Yorkshire players were made honorary life members of the club?

847 Who was J.M. Kilburn's successor as *Yorkshire Post* cricket correspondent?

848 Who was reappointed Yorkshire captain in 1986?

849 Which former Yorkshire and England Captain had the name "Dransfield" as one of his first names?

850 Who completed the "double" in his first season for Yorkshire in 1949?

851 Name the three Yorkshire players to tour India in 1963-64.

852 In 1974, who performed the hat-trick against Notts at Worksop?

853 Who are these two cricketers in festive mood?

854 An unfamiliar picture of a former Yorkshire ground. Where is it?

855 A famous old pavilion – alas, no more – where is it?

856 Hedley Verity Memorial Match in 1945. Where was it played?

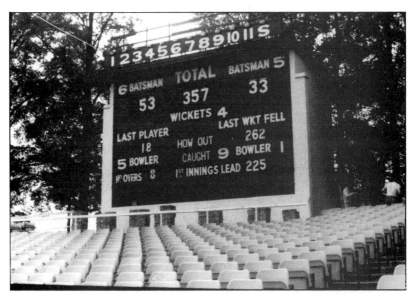

857 View of old Headingley scoreboard. What is of significance?

858 Who is the cricketer depicted?

859 Who is this cricketer?

860 Who is this cricketer?

861 Where is this?

862 Where are these cricket gates and who does one associate with them?

863 The Kilners are the only pair of brothers to have recorded centuries for Yorkshire. True or False?

864 Chris Balderstone played soccer for Brechin City. True or False?

865 J.B. Priestley's father played League cricket in the Bradford area. True or False?

866 General Booth was a leading Yorkshire all-rounder before the War. True or False?

867 The Brontë family were related to Ephraim Lockwood. True or False?

868 Sir Everard Radcliffe was the second successive Captain of Yorkshire not to have been born in the County. True or False?

869 Mike Brearley's father played for Yorkshire. True or False?

870 John Tunnicliffe was born in Kent. True or False?

871 David Hunter was an expert on canaries, clog-dancing and bell-ringing. True or False?

872 Jack Van Geloven was the only Dutchman to play for Yorkshire. True or False?

ANCIENT HISTORY

873 Who kept the Adelphi Hotel in Sheffield where the Yorkshire C.C.C. was founded?

874 What was his claim to cricket fame?

875 Who was the first?

876 What was his claim to fame?

877 What was the highest score by a Yorkshire player in the nineteenth century?

878 Who made that score?

879 Who was the first Englishman to score over 400 runs in a Test series v. Australia?

880 Who was Yorkshire's first noted wicket-keeper before the County club was formed?

881 Who was known as "The Star of the North" and was knocked down and killed by a railway train near Rochdale station?

882 Two well-known Huddersfield League clubs were known as cricket nurseries in the early days of Yorkshire cricket. One was Lascelles Hall. Name the other.

LEAGUE CLUBS – I

With which cricket Leagues do you associate the following Yorkshire clubs?

883 Barnby Dun

884 Kirkheaton

885 Pickering

886 York

887 East Bierley

888 Woodhouse

889 Pateley Bridge

890 Hull

891 Yorkshire Main

892 Shadwell

893 Redcar

894 Millhouses

895 Pudsey St Lawrence

896 Sowerby St Peters

897 Lascelles Hall

898 Hull Zingari

899 Gildersome

PERCY HOLMES

900 Where and when was he born?

901 How many times did he open for England against Australia?

902 How many appearances did he make for England in Test cricket?

903 How many centuries did he score for Yorkshire?

904 How many centuries did he score in first-class cricket?
905 What was his highest Test innings?
906 How many times did he score 2,000 runs in a season?

HERBERT SUTCLIFFE

907 How many Test Matches did he play in?
908 What was his highest Test score?
909 Where did it take place and in what year?
910 How many seasons did he open the innings with Holmes?
911 His son Billy, who captained Yorkshire, had as one of his forenames the name of a famous cricketer. What was that name?

TEST PLAYERS – I

912 How many Yorkshire cricketers have represented England?
913 How many captained England?
914 How many were amateurs?
915 Name those amateurs.
916 How many were related?
917 Name the pair of brothers.
918 Name the father and son.
919 Who played in the most Tests?
920 How many did he play in?
921 How many centuries did Sutcliffe, Hutton and Boycott score between them?
922 Apart from Sutcliffe, who had the highest overall batting average?
923 How many took 100 wickets in Tests?
924 Name the four apart from Trueman and Rhodes.
925 There were eight wicket-keepers amongst them, but two were not regular wicket-keepers for Yorkshire. Name them.
926 Which regular Yorkshire wicket-keeper kept wicket in most matches for England?

927 Where was this picture taken?
928 Who is the wicket-keeper?
929 Who is the player immediately behind him?
930 Who is the player on his right?

Can you identify the following ties?

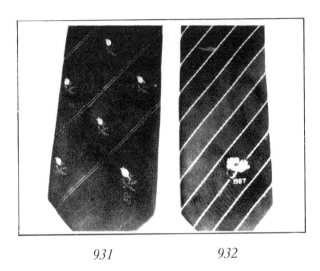

931   932

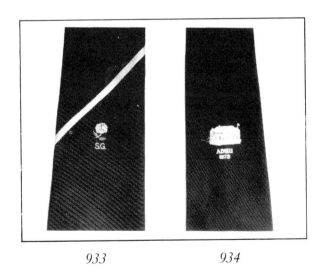

933   934

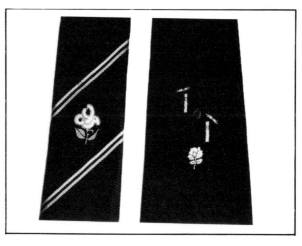

935   936

LEAGUE CLUBS – 2

With which cricket Leagues do you associate the following Yorkshire clubs?

937 Otley
938 Keighley Technical College
939 Goole
940 Sheffield United
941 Collingham
942 Bowling Old Lane
943 Tinsley
944 Todmorden
945 Whiston Parish Church
946 Bentley
947 Delph and Dobcross
948 Ackworth

949 Northallerton
950 Tadcaster
951 Dewsbury
952 Saltburn
953 Sessay
954 Greenfield
955 Fenners
956 Idle

GREAT NAMES IN LEAGUE CRICKET

957 Perhaps the greatest bowler in the game's history; he played several seasons with a Bradford League club. His name, please?

958 Which club did he play for?

959 Which famous England player played for Saltaire as a junior?

960 A great Yorkshire and England batsman used to open the innings with Edgar Oldroyd. Name him.

961 Which cricket club did they play for?

962 Hardly a word to associate with John Berry Hobbs but he played for this club during the Great War. Name the club.

963 Before he played for Yorkshire, Hedley Verity played in League cricket in Lancashire. Which two Lancashire clubs did he play with?

964 Which was the club in Yorkshire that Verity learned his cricket with?

965 With which Bradford League club did Learie Constantine play?

966 Frank Woolley performed well with which Bradford League club during the Great War?

967 This famous Lancashire batsman played with a Pudsey club in 1916. Who was he?

968 Name the club.

969 Which Yorkshire and England all-rounder went to be a professional at Walsall after he retired from first-class cricket?

970 Who were the only pair of brothers to have played for Yorkshire, both having been born outside the County?

971 Who scored two centuries in a match for Yorkshire more times than any other player?

972 How many times did he perform the feat?

973 How many times has the feat been performed for Yorkshire?

974 Who was the last player to perform the feat?

975 There have been 21 partnerships of 300 or more in the annals of Yorkshire cricket. Which batsman has been associated in more of these partnerships than any other batsman?

976 Which was the last 300 partnership for Yorkshire and when?

977 Who was it against and who were the partners?

978 When did Boycott last take part in a 300 stand for Yorkshire?

979 How many left-arm slow bowlers have taken 1,000 wickets for Yorkshire?

980 Name three other left-arm slow bowlers who took over 500 wickets for Yorkshire.

981 Name the three Yorkshire left-hand bats to exceed 20,000 runs for Yorkshire.

982 How many left-handed batsmen who played regularly averaged over forty for Yorkshire?

TEST PLAYERS - 2

983 When did P.A. Gibb first keep wicket for England?

984 Of the players who played in ten Tests or more, which of them had the highest ratio of catches per match?

985 What was this average?

986 Who else had an average of more than one per match?

987 Which bowler averaged 119.00?

988 Which bowler averaged 109.00?

989 Which bowler with ten wickets or more had the poorest average?

990 Which batsman scored 161 against South Africa?
991 Which batsman twice scored 161 against Australia?
992 Who scored exactly 100 on four occasions?
993 How many batsmen scored over 200 in a Test innings?
994 Name them.
995 How many times did Boycott score over 200?
996 How many times did Hutton score over 200?
997 Who took four wickets in five balls v. Pakistan at Birmingham in 1978?
998 Who took 14 wickets in a day in a Test Match v. Australia in 1934 at Lord's?
999 Who is the only English cricketer to have appeared in a Test Match for England before his nineteenth birthday?

LEAGUE CLUBS – 3

With which cricket Leagues do you associate the following Yorkshire clubs?

1000 Adel
1001 Thorp Arch and Boston Spa
1002 Lepton
1003 Malton
1004 Bedale
1005 Darfield
1006 Wakefield
1007 Wombwell
1008 Slaithwaite
1009 Driffield
1010 Shiregreen
1011 Sykehouse
1012 Grimethorpe
1013 Settle
1014 Armthorpe Welfare
1015 North Leeds
1016 Earby
1017 Sheffield Bankers

1018 Brecks
1019 Skipton Church Institute
1020 Heckmondwike
1021 Stainborough
1022 Eastrington
1023 Cleckheaton
1024 East Leeds
1025 Skipton
1026 Treeton Welfare
1027 Copley

Answers

TEST MATCHES - I

1   R.T. Stanyforth
2   N.W.D. Yardley
3   R. Illingworth
4   L. Hutton
5   F. Mitchell
6   Hon. F.S. Jackson
7   P.A. Gibb
8   J.T. Brown senior
9   F.S. Trueman
10   R. Peel

YORKSHIRE CAPTAINS

11   A.B. Sellers
12   J.V. Wilson
13   J.R. Burnet
14   W.H.H. Sutcliffe
15   N.W.D. Yardley
16   John Hampshire
17   Sir William Worsley
18   Sir E.J. Radcliffe
19   C.M. Old
20   D.B. Close

SIR LEONARD HUTTON IN TEST CRICKET

21   In 1950 at Old Trafford
22   1950-51 in Adelaide
23   Five
24   1948-49
25   None
26   Two
27   One
28   J.H. Parks

29   Batted at number 5
30   R.R. Lindwall

UMPIRES PAST AND PRESENT

31   D. Denton
32   A. Dolphin
33   John Hampshire
34   H.D. Bird
35   J. Birkenshaw
36   Emmott Robinson
37   Chris Balderstone
38   Barrie Leadbeater
39   Syd Buller
40   G.P. Harrison

CONNECTIONS ABROAD

41   Hubert Myers
42   Ken Taylor
43   I. Washington
44   Frank Mitchell
45   J.H. Hampshire

CAPS AND EMBLEMS

46   White
47   11
48   Cambridge blue, Oxford blue and gold
49   Lord Hawke
50   S.D. Fletcher and P.E. Robinson

DIFFICULT AUTHORS

51   B.B. Wilson
52   Ray Illingworth

80 Eight
81 168
82 15
83 Five times
84 68
85 28
86 1,251
87 1,351
88 Kettering
89 M.C.C.
90 Six for 33
91 West Indies, 1939 at Old Trafford
92 Arthur Wood
93 1933, Auckland, against New Zealand
94 All bowled
95 W.R. Hammond scored 336

PICTURE QUIZ – I

96 Lord Hawke, J.T. Brown senior
97 S. Haigh, G.H. Hirst and W. Rhodes
98 D. Hunter
99 Arthur Sellers
100 1908
101 W.H. Wilkinson
102 W.E. Bates
103 Major Booth
104 Alonzo Drake
105 Sir Archibald White

DAVID BAIRSTOW

106 At Chesterfield v. Derbyshire in 1973
107 At Trent Bridge in 1988
108 He took a G.C.E. examination on the morning of the
    match.

109 Glamorgan
110 At Middlesbrough in 1976
111 Roger Tolchard
112 He took 11 catches, which equalled the world record for the number of catches taken in one match.
113 Arnold Long and Rodney Marsh
114 Catches held in one innings by a Yorkshire wicket-keeper
115 First Yorkshire wicket-keeper to take six dismissals in an innings three times.

R. ILLINGWORTH

116 Pudsey, 8 June 1932
117 18 August 1951 v. Hampshire at Headingley
118 Leicestershire
119 1969-78
120 W. Watson
121 1973
122 In 1957 at Worcester
123 1970-71
124 v. Essex at Chelmsford in 1983
125 The John Player Special League

1946 SEASON

126 First
127 A.B. Sellers
128 H. Verity, H. Sutcliffe and A. Mitchell
129 Arthur Booth
130 L. Hutton and W. Barber
131 Seven
132 Somerset at Taunton
133 Hutton, Gibb, Smailes and Bowes
134 It was discovered after two overs that the pitch was 24 yards long.
135 E.P. Robinson

136 They were brothers

137 1930

138 G. Boycott and G. B. Stevenson

139 A.W. Pullin

140 A cricket writer

141 A time limit match took place

142 221 v. Kent in 1921

143 Hon. F.S. Jackson

144 D. Byas and P. J. Berry

145 G. Boycott and G. B. Stevenson

146 204*

147 Scarborough

148 G. Boycott

149 Thomas Lord

150 N.W.D. Yardley

151 E.I. Lester 125* and 132

152 Vic Wilson (1960)

153 M. Coope (53); J. Lawrence (6 for 35)

154 L. Hutton (269)

155 R. Illingworth, 7 for 58 and 7 for 6

156 G.A. Cope and C.M. Old

157 It happened in the month when he obtained the record aggregate for one month (June)

158 D.B. Close, M.J. Cowan and W.H.H. Sutcliffe

159 A.G. Nicholson 9 for 62

160 C.M. Old

161 P. Carrick

162 Sir Leonard Hutton

163 R. Appleyard

164 H.D. Bird and P.N. Broughton

165 Because the match had been won by Yorkshire on the Sunday

YORKSHIRE GENTLEMEN

166 H.D. Badger

167 Joseph Frank
168 A.T. Barber
169 Lord Hawke
170 Capt. W.E. Blackburn
171 J.A. Richardson
172 Horace Brearley
173 J.P. Wilson
174 Revd E.S. Carter
175 Revd C.M. Sharpe

MISCELLANEOUS – I

176 George Britton
177 Brian Close
178 Rugby Union
179 George Hirst
180 Len Hutton for obstructing the field in 1951 against South Africa
181 R. Peel, 3
182 F.S. Trueman
183 21
184 Howdenshire 1915-26
185 Five

YORKSHIRE GROUNDS

186 St George's Road
187 Castle Hill
188 Fartown (St John's Ground)
189 Thrum Hall
190 Bramall Lane
191 North Marine Road
192 The Circle (Anlaby Road)
193 Headingley
194 Park Avenue
195 Acklam Park

PICTURE QUIZ - 2

196 G. Wilson
197 D.C.F. Burton
198 Percy Holmes
199 Edgar Oldroyd
200 Herbert Sutcliffe and Percy Holmes
201 At Leyton in 1932
202 Bramall Lane
203 George Macaulay and Major Lupton
204 Emmott Robinson and Maurice Leyland
205 A Yorkshire cap and a Yorkshire 2nd XI cap

BIRTHPLACES - I

206 Redcar
207 Keighley
208 Stairfoot, Barnsley
209 Horsforth
210 Armley, Leeds
211 Huddersfield
212 Keighley
213 Leeds
214 Bradford
215 Hemsworth

FIRSTS

216 H. Fisher v. Somerset at Sheffield in 1932
217 C. Tyson v. Hampshire at Southampton in 1921
218 W. Rhodes
219 L. Hutton
220 W. Bates at Melbourne, 1882-83
221 F.S. Trueman
222 J.H. Hampshire v. West Indies at Lord's, 1969
223 G. Boycott at Nottingham, 1977

224 G. G. Macaulay v. South Africa in 1923 at Cape Town
225 G. Ulyett v. Australia at Melbourne 1882

NICKNAMES – EASY

226 Chilly
227 Blue (or Stan)
228 Sawdust
229 Ticker
230 Lavender
231 Lucky
232 Dickie
233 Sandy
234 Happy Jack
235 Bingo

DATES

236 1934
237 1893
238 1956
239 1863
240 1932
241 1932
242 1977
243 1939
244 1901
245 1966

MISCELLANEOUS – 2

246 Bramall Lane, Sheffield
247 Bill Bowes
248 D.C.F. Burton
249 J.H. Nash

250 Wilfred Rhodes

251 Hull

252 Both hit the ball over the houses into Trafalgar Square at Scarborough

253 G. Boycott

254 H. Sutcliffe

255 W.H.H. Sutcliffe

256 H. Sutcliffe

257 J.A. Cowie

258 L. Hutton (82)

259 Alonzo Drake

260 F.W. Milligan

BIRTHPLACES – 2

261 C.H. Parkin

262 Lord Hawke

263 W.G. Keighley

264 F.W. Milligan

265 Revd H.M. Sims

266 J.P. Whitehead

267 R.T. Stanyforth

268 G.A. Smithson

269 Revd William Law

270 Capt. W.E. Blackburn

NICKNAMES – DIFFICULT

271 Old Tarpot

272 Mary Anne

273 Old Ironsides

274 Tiddley-Push

275 The Marquis

276 The Duke

277 The Dormouse

278 Gnasher

279 Teapot
280 Turkey

281 Percy Holmes
282 Hedley Verity
283 They had not qualified to play in it because they were third
284 Norfolk
285 Not decided or null and void – declared to be "undecided"
286 Yorkshire Gentlemen
287 Alec Coxon
288 W. Rhodes, H. Sutcliffe and M. Leyland
289 F.A. Lowson and D.B. Close
290 A. Ramage
291 Ellis P. Robinson
292 T.L. Taylor
293 D.V. Brennan
294 D.E.V. Padgett
295 G. Boycott

PICTURE QUIZ – 3

296 Cecil Tyson
297 Tong Park
298 Arthur Dolphin
299 Sir William Worsley
300 Len Hutton, Frank Smailes, Bill Bowes and Ellis Robinson
301 Wilf Barber is presenting the Tanner Cup at Moorside, Oldham in 1946, to Austerlands skipper Syd Belshaw.
302 J.P. Wilson
303 Barber and Hutton
304 At Scarborough in 1946
305 Fartown, Huddersfield

AFTER THE GREAT WAR – 1919 SEASON

306 D.C.F. Burton

307 1907

308 Twenty-six

309 First

310 Two-day matches from 11.30 a.m. to 7.30 p.m.

311 Highest percentage of wins to matches played

312 Herbert Sutcliffe

313 Sutcliffe, Holmes and Denton

314 W. Rhodes

315 W. Rhodes (147)

RELATIONS

316 Nephew and uncle

317 Uncle and nephew

318 Father and son

319 Brothers

320 Nephew and uncle

321 Father and son

322 Father and son

323 Brothers

324 Uncle and nephew

325 Uncle and nephew

JOHN PLAYER SPECIAL LEAGUE

326 Bradford, Scarborough, Hull, Leeds, Middlesbrough, Harrogate, Huddersfield, Sheffield (Bramall Lane and Abbeydale Park)

327 23 by Middlesex at Headingley, 1974

328 P.W. Jarvis at Derby v. Derbyshire, 1982

329 Richard Hutton 7 for 15 v. Worcestershire, Leeds in 1969

330 A.G. Nicholson in 1974

BOWLERS

331 Slow left arm
332 Left arm medium fast
333 Right arm fast
334 Slow left arm
335 Left arm medium fast
336 Right arm medium fast/off-breaks
337 Right arm leg breaks
338 Right arm off-breaks
339 Right arm off-breaks
340 Right arm medium fast

BATSMEN

341 Leyland
342 Vic Wilson
343 W.H. Wilkinson
344 Washington
345 Stott
346 Kevin Sharp
347 Watson
348 Birkenshaw
349 None of them
350 Hatton

TEST MATCHES – 2

351 Aged 41
352 67 by New Zealand in 1958
353 1899
354 584 by Australia in 1934
355 At Edgbaston
356 P. Roy, M.K. Mantri and V.L. Manjrekar
357 F.S. Trueman
358 R. Illingworth

359 L. Hutton and W. Watson
360 W. Watson (116)
361 He took 5 for 58 and 6 for 30 and effectively won the match for his side. In the second innings he had a spell of 5 for 0.

COUNTY CHAMPIONSHIP

362 1867
363 1869 and 1949
364 Nottinghamshire 1869, Middlesex 1949
365 17th
366 In 1983
367 31
368 12
369 1968
370 1926 and 1928
371 1953, when they lost as many as they won

WILFRED RHODES – I

372 Galashiels
373 1899 at Trent Bridge
374 W.G. Grace
375 Kirkheaton
376 M.C.C. at Lord's, 12 May 1898

F.S. JACKSON

377 Chapel Allerton, Leeds
378 1939-47
379 1921
380 Winston Churchill
381 He won the toss in every Test and topped both batting and bowling averages

CHAMPIONSHIP WINNERS

382 1924
383 1968
384 1893
385 1938
386 1923
387 1946
388 1959
389 1919
390 1908
391 1935

PICTURE QUIZ – 4

392 Ken Smales
393 Johnny Wardle
394 Ron Aspinall
395 Ted Lester
396 Gerry Smithson
397 Don Brennan
398 Harry Halliday
399 Headingley
400 Don Wilson
401 Stott and Bird

AUSTRALIAN TESTS

402 F.S. Jackson
403 G.H. Hirst (35)
404 M. Leyland
405 H. Sutcliffe (436)
406 H. Verity
407 W. Rhodes
408 A. Hill
409 A. Hill

410 T. Emmett
411 H. Carter and A. Dolphin

1938

412 Bowes, Hutton, Leyland, Gibb, Smailes, Verity and Wood
413 Seven
414 M. Leyland
415 L. Hutton
416 Lord Hawke
417 In the first innings Gibb retired hurt, and in the second innings Hutton and Gibb were absent injured and Leyland retired hurt.
418 E.W. Whitfield
419 P.A. Gibb, 79, Cambridge; E.J.H. Dixon, 108, Oxford
420 K.R. Davidson
421 Bowes, Robinson, Smailes and Verity

A WET SEASON – 1958

422 Brian Statham 6 for 16
423 George Tribe 7 for 22 and 8 for 9
424 R.V.C. Robins
425 P.B.H. May
426 G.A.R. Lock
427 R. Illingworth
428 David Pickles
429 W. Watson
430 F.S. Trueman and D. Wilson
431 E.I. Lester

SCHOFIELD HAIGH

432 1,916
433 9 for 25 v. Gloucester at Leeds in 1912

434 Four
435 Berry Brow, Huddersfield
436 Coach at Winchester
437 Three times
438 11,099
439 1895
440 South Africa – 1898-99
441 Lord Hawke

WILFRED RHODES - 2

442 1903-04 Australia
443 Sir Pelham Warner
444 2,325
445 31,156
446 3,608
447 1930
448 23
449 267* v. Leicestershire in 1921 at Headingley
450 20 times
451 C.A. Roach
452 Kingston, Jamaica on 10 April 1930. It was the seventh day of the match.
453 Three times
454 Not once; but he was dropped off him three times in the match v. Leveson Gower's XI at Scarborough.
455 Albert Trott
456 One, v. Thornton's XI, Scarborough

MISCELLANEOUS - 4

457 Because the pitch had been doctored during the preceding night
458 Louis Hall
459 14 times
460 The Australians

461 The South Africans
462 W. Ringrose
463 J.V. Wilson
464 Yorkshire combined with Lancashire to play against the Australians
465 Hull and Old Trafford
466 Derbyshire at Sheffield
467 J.H. Hampshire (158)
468 Glamorgan at Swansea
469 D.V. Brennan, P.A. Gibb and R.T. Stanyforth
470 F.A. Lowson
471 R. Illingworth

1980 SEASON

472 A. Sidebottom, C.W.J. Athey and J.D. Love
473 H. Sutcliffe
474 John Hampshire
475 50 (46 caught, 4 stumped)
476 G.A. Cope and B. Leadbeater

PICTURE QUIZ – 5

477 David Pickles
478 R. Illingworth
479 J. Birkenshaw
480 Brian Close
481 Vic Wilson
482 Bryan Stott
483 Brian Bolus
484 Phil Sharpe
485 Mike Cowan
486 Ronnie Burnet

487 B. Leadbeater
488 J.D. Love
489 C.M. Old
490 A.B. Sellers
491 Nine
492 He was the first Yorkshire player to score centuries in his first two home matches
493 C. Lethbridge
494 Neil Hartley
495 Bob Taylor
496 Paul W. Jarvis

CRICKET AUTHORS

497 Norman Yardley
498 Len Hutton
499 Willie Watson
500 Geoff Boycott
501 Len Hutton
502 John Hampshire
503 H.D. Bird
504 Lord Hawke
505 Cecil Parkin
506 Phil Sharpe

PUBLIC SCHOOLS

507 St Peter's School, York
508 Rugby (or Winchester, where he taught for many years)
509 Coach at Harrow
510 Shrewsbury (or Ludgrove, where he was headmaster for many years)
511 Downside
512 St Peter's School, York

513 Eton
514 Harrow
515 Eton
516 Coach at Eton

ASSOCIATIONS

517 J. Tunnicliffe
518 Rhodes
519 Herbert Sutcliffe
520 George Freeman (or Allan Hill)
521 George Ulyett
522 I. Hodgson
523 A. Drake
524 K. Taylor
525 Hirst (and Rhodes)
526 Len Hutton

NUMBERS

527 F.S. Trueman
528 G.H. Hirst
529 W. Rhodes
530 L. Hutton
531 L. Hutton
532 H. Verity
533 Holmes and Sutcliffe
534 L. Hutton
535 H. Sutcliffe
536 Brown and Tunnicliffe
537 G. Boycott
538 G.H. Hirst
539 G. Boycott
540 H. Verity
541 G.H. Hirst

CUP COMPETITIONS

542 The Bradford League
543 Airedale and Wharfedale League
544 The Huddersfield League
545 The Leeds League
546 North Yorkshire and South Durham League
547 Central Yorkshire League
548 Pontefract Section (Yorks Council)
549 Halifax League (and District)
550 Sheffield Cricket League
551 Wetherby Cricket League

MISCELLANEOUS – 5

552 F. Mitchell
553 Assistant Secretary of Yorkshire C.C.C.
554 1933
555 1964
556 Australia at The Oval
557 R.T. Stanyforth
558 Badminton
559 Roy Kilner
560 R. Illingworth
561 R.P. Hodson
562 J.G. Binks
563 107 in 1960
564 96 catches – a record for one season
565 Hedley Verity
566 Alfred Austin

1988 SEASON

567 Three
568 P.E. Robinson
569 A. Sidebottom

570 Metcalfe and Byas
571 A.A. Metcalfe
572 F.D. Stephenson
573 P. Carrick
574 M.D. Moxon
575 East Bierley
576 Scarborough
577 Nostell St Oswald
578 Barnsley
579 Eighth
580 Gerald Howat
581 Sir Leonard Hutton
582 D. Ripley and S.J. Rhodes
583 C.W.J. Athey
584 M.A. Robinson
585 M.K. Bore
586 N.A. Mallender

PICTURE QUIZ – 6

587 Binks and Illingworth
588 Tony Nicholson
589 S.D. Fletcher, G.B. Stevenson, S.J. Rhodes
590 Doug Padgett
591 Stephen Rhodes and Paul Jarvis
592 Barrie Leadbeater and Geoff Cope, Yorkshire beneficiaries
593 Kevin Sharp
594 Martyn Moxon
595 Arthur Mitchell
596 Reg Allen

A MIXED BAG

597 L. Hutton
598 L. Hutton and F.S. Trueman
599 Hutton scored 104, Trueman took 8 for 31 in the first
    innings

600 R. Illingworth
601 R.K. Platt and D. Wilson
602 He had to bat with one arm, having broken his thumb
603 26
604 Surrey at the Oval in 1909
605 G.A. Cope
606 H.P. Cooper
607 G. Boycott
608 L. Hutton (201) at Old Trafford
609 J.H. Wardle
610 R. Appleyard
611 J.H. Wardle

SCHOOLS – PRESENT-DAY ASSOCIATIONS

612 Rydal
613 St Peter's School, York
614 Bootham
615 Repton
616 Shrewsbury
617 St Edward's, Oxford
618 Ashville College
619 Cheltenham
620 Leeds Grammar School
621 Bedford Modern School

SCHOOLS – PAST ASSOCIATIONS

622 Wellington
623 Barnard Castle
624 Eton
625 St Peter's School, York
626 Uppingham

E. WAINWRIGHT

627 7 May 1888 v. M.C.C. at Lord's
628 v. Australians at Bradford, 27 June 1888
629 Right-arm off-breaks
630 Tinsley, near Sheffield
631 228, v. Surrey at the Oval, 1899
632 Australia at Lord's, 17 July 1893
633 Five
634 Once in 1897
635 Worksop C.C.
636 Neville Cardus

FOOTBALL CLUBS – I

637 Holbeck
638 Leeds United at Elland Road
639 Fartown
640 Headingley
641 Bradford Park Avenue
642 Sheffield United's ground at Bramall Lane
643 York City's ground at Bootham Crescent
644 Hull – The Circle
645 Acklam Park, Middlesbrough
646 Abbeydale Park, Sheffield

YORKSHIRE EXILES – I

647 Northants
648 Leicestershire
649 Warwickshire
650 Worcestershire
651 Warwickshire
652 Lancashire
653 Glamorgan
654 Warwickshire

655 Glamorgan
656 Worcestershire

EXILES WITH TWO COUNTIES

657 Leicestershire and Worcestershire
658 Lancashire and Derbyshire
659 Nottinghamshire and Derbyshire
660 Northumberland and Durham

PICTURE QUIZ – 7

661 Paul Gibb
662 Kirkheaton
663 Saltaire – the Bradford League champions
664 "Dickie" Bird
665 Chris Balderstone
666 Fartown, Huddersfield
667 Willie Watson and Bob Appleyard
668 Scarborough
669 Billy Sutcliffe
670 Headingley, v. Lancs., 1956

FOOTBALL CLUBS – 2

671 Manchester United, Huddersfield Town and Halifax
     Town
672 Middlesbrough and Derby County
673 Huddersfield Town, Doncaster Rovers, Carlisle United and
     Queen of the South
674 Bradford City and Halifax Town
675 Bradford City
676 Huddersfield Town and Bradford Park Avenue
677 Barnsley, Swansea Town, Portsmouth
678 Bradford City

679 Huddersfield Town, Sunderland and Halifax Town
680 Sheffield United
681 Sheffield United
682 Sheffield United, Sheffield Wednesday and Middlesbrough
683 Sheffield Wednesday, Derby County, Bolton Wanderers and Burnley
684 Leeds City
685 Rotherham Town
686 York City

MISCELLANEOUS – 6

687 Paul Gibb
688 H.P. Cooper and G.A. Cope
689 E.R. Wilson
690 A.J. Webbe's XI (in 1899)
691 John Tunnicliffe
692 Yorkshire
693 1966-68
694 Northamptonshire
695 Leicestershire, Fartown
696 R. Illingworth, A.G. Nicholson, F.S. Trueman and D. Wilson
697 Scarborough
698 G.H. Hirst
699 G. Boycott
700 W. Watson
701 Alan Jones
702 Bowled out Yorkshire for 31
703 In 1981
704 D.V. Brennan, E. Leadbeater and F.A. Lowson
705 Partly due to the fact that the Duke was Patron of Kent C.C.C. and the Duchess was Patroness of Yorkshire C.C.C.
706 S. Oldham and B. Wood
707 M.K. Bore
708 F.C. Toone

709 Andrew Townsley
710 J.V. Wilson
711 Billy Bates (grandfather of Ted Bates)
712 Sir Kenneth Parkinson
713 All Secretaries of the Yorkshire C.C.C.
714 Colin Johnson
715 J.T. Brown senior
716 Bob Andrew

1948

717 N.W.D. Yardley
718 Frank Smailes
719 Fourth
720 Hutton, Halliday, Lester and Watson
721 M.C.C. and the Australians
722 E.I. Lester
723 Barnes, Bradman (2), Brown, Harvey and Morris
724 M.P. Donnelly
725 George Pope
726 E.H. Edrich (121)

GEORGE HERBERT HIRST

727 341, v. Leicester in 1905
728 14
729 56
730 1904
731 £3,703
732 Roy Kilner (£4,016)
733 Left-arm medium fast
734 v. Gloucestershire at Bristol in 1894
735 A.E. Stoddart's team to Australia in 1897-98
736 152.00

737 Leicestershire
738 Worcestershire
739 Gloucestershire
740 Warwickshire
741 Worcestershire
742 Derbyshire
743 Nottinghamshire
744 Nottinghamshire
745 Nottinghamshire
746 Somerset

1988

747 Brian Close
748 Brian Walsh
749 J. Lister
750 Peter Townend
751 Viscount Mountgarret
752 John Featherstone
753 Neil Hartley
754 David Hopps
755 David Warner
756 John Callaghan
757 Robert Mills
758 Leeds Cricket, Football and Athletic Club
759 The Abbeydale Sports Club
760 HRH The Duchess of Kent
761 Jimmy Binks

PICTURE QUIZ – 8

762 Peter Hartley
763 Ted Lester, Mike Cowan
764 The Herbert Sutcliffe gates at Headingley

765 The pavilion, Acklam Park, Middlesbrough
766 Stuart Fletcher
767 Martyn Moxon
768 Acklam Park (note the rugby posts)
769 Richard Blakey
770 Arthur Robinson
771 George Cawthray

UMPIRES – 2

772 Balderstone, Bird, Hampshire, Leadbeater and Birkenshaw
773 Ron Aspinall
774 B. Leadbeater
775 Peter Rochford
776 Louis Hall

TEST MATCHES – 3

777 R. Appleyard
778 N.W.D. Yardley
779 W. Bates (1882-83)
780 George Ulyett
781 Wilfred Rhodes

PROBLEMS

782 H. Sedgwick in 1906 v. Worcestershire
783 He did the hat-trick
784 There were none
785 D.B. Close
786 Eric Burgin
787 G.H. Hirst (1904)
788 Arthur Booth
789 C.C. Clifford (24)
790 Brian Close's wife's maiden name
791 Bradford Park Avenue

G. BOYCOTT

792 Lord's, July 1981, Australia
793 1971 and 1979
794 1971
795 Four
796 48,426
797 56.83
798 Nottinghamshire, Sheffield (1966) and Bradford, (1983)
799 11 August 1977
800 Graham Roope
801 Australia
802 Greg Chappell
803 17 before him
804 New Zealand in 1966
805 2,221 runs
806 105.76
807 103
808 22
809 Wakefield
810 Five (he played in only a few matches in 1962)
811 2 October 1963
812 Run out

FRED TRUEMAN

813 67
814 Neil Hawke
815 Colin Cowdrey
816 Len Hutton
817 Cambridge University
818 11 May 1949
819 N.W.D. Yardley
820 Frank Lowson and Brian Close
821 Notts
822 M.C.C.
823 It was performed before lunch

824 For England v. Young England in 1963
825 Hubert Doggart
826 Umrigar
827 Craven
828 1960
829 Neath (in 1954)
830 South Africans (in 1951)
831 Schofield Haigh
832 None

MISCELLANEOUS - 7

833 Don Wilson
834 Peter Ingham
835 Left-arm slow
836 Topped first-class bowling averages
837 Brian Close
838 Alonzo Drake
839 R. Peel
840 Robin Jackman
841 A. Wood 123* v. Worcestershire in 1935
842 R.D. Jackman and Intikhab Alam
843 Neil Smith
844 G.B. Stevenson
845 The Oval, 16 July 1951
846 F.S. Trueman and N.W.D. Yardley
847 Terry Brindle
848 D.L. Bairstow
849 N.W.D. Yardley
850 D.B. Close
851 J.G. Binks, P.J. Sharpe and D. Wilson
852 A.L. Robinson

PICTURE QUIZ - 9

853 Emmott Robinson and Edgar Oldroyd
854 Dewsbury

855 Park Avenue, Bradford
856 Roundhay Park, Leeds
857 Taken on 5 June 1981, at completion of drawn match with Essex after which the scoreboard was dismantled and replaced by an electronic scoreboard.
858 Schofield Haigh
859 T.L. Taylor
860 H. Sutcliffe
861 The Boycott gates at the entrance to Ackworth C.C., where Geoffrey played as a boy.
862 Primrose Hill, Ken Taylor

TRUE OR FALSE?

863 True
864 False
865 True
866 False
867 False
868 True
869 True
870 True (not the county, but a district of Pudsey)
871 True
872 False

ANCIENT HISTORY

873 Harry Sampson
874 He was a well-known Sheffield and Yorkshire batsman and the second player to appear for Players v. Gentlemen from Yorkshire.
875 Tom Marsden
876 Scored 227 against Nottingham in 1826
877 311
878 J.T. Brown senior, v. Sussex in 1897
879 G. Ulyett

880 George Chatterton
881 Thomas Hunt
882 Dalton

LEAGUE CLUBS – I

883 Doncaster
884 Huddersfield
885 East Yorkshire Cup
886 Yorkshire
887 Bradford
888 Leeds
889 Nidderdale
890 Yorkshire
891 Doncaster
892 Wetherby
893 North Yorkshire and South Durham
894 Sheffield
895 Bradford
896 Halifax
897 Huddersfield
898 East Yorkshire Cup
899 Central Yorkshire

PERCY HOLMES

900 Oakes, Huddersfield – 25 November 1886
901 Once
902 Seven
903 60
904 67
905 88
906 Seven

HERBERT SUTCLIFFE

907 54

908 194

909 Sydney – in 1932

910 15

911 Hobbs

TEST PLAYERS – I

912 65

913 Eight

914 Four

915 Lord Hawke and Hon. F.S. Jackson, R.T. Stanyforth and N.W.D.Yardley

916 Two brothers and a father and son

917 C.E.M. Wilson and E.R. Wilson

918 L. Hutton and R.A. Hutton

919 G. Boycott

920 108

921 57

922 L. Hutton (56.67)

923 Six

924 H. Verity, J.H. Wardle, R. Peel and R. Illingworth

925 P.A. Gibb and R.T. Stanyforth

926 J. Hunter

PICTURE QUIZ – 10

927 Ampleforth College

928 D.V. Brennan

929 Billy Sutcliffe

930 Len Hutton (F.S. Trueman and D.E.V. Padgett are also in the photograph)

PICTURE QUIZ – 11

931 Colin Johnson Appreciation Fund tie
932 Yorkshire C.C.C. benefit tie, 1987
933 Yorkshire C.C.C., Southern Group tie
934 Adieu Bramall Lane tie, 1973
935 Yorkshire Cricket Association tie
936 Tykes on Tour tie

LEAGUE CLUBS – 2

937 Airedale and Wharfedale
938 Craven
939 Humber-Don
940 Yorkshire
941 Wetherby
942 Bradford
943 Sheffield
944 Lancashire
945 South Riding
946 Humber-Don
947 Saddleworth
948 Pontefract
949 North Yorkshire and South Durham
950 York Senior
951 Central Yorkshire
952 North Yorkshire and South Durham
953 York Senior
954 Saddleworth
955 Humber-Don
956 Bradford

GREAT NAMES IN LEAGUE CRICKET

957 Sydney F. Barnes
958 Saltaire

959 J.C. Laker
960 L. Hutton
961 Pudsey St Lawrence
962 Idle
963 Accrington and Middleton
964 Rawdon
965 Windhill
966 Keighley
967 E. Tyldesley
968 Pudsey Britannia
969 Frank Smailes

GENERAL

970 The Suggs (W. and F.H.)
971 L. Hutton
972 Three times
973 15
974 M.D. Moxon
975 H. Sutcliffe – nine
976 351 in 1985
977 Worcestershire; Boycott and Moxon
978 Never before that
979 Five
980 R. Kilner, E. Peate and P. Carrick
981 M. Leyland, D.B. Close and J.V. Wilson
982 One – M. Leyland

TEST PLAYERS – 2

983 Against India in 1946
984 P.J. Sharpe
985 1.416
986 D.B. Close 1.090 and W. Rhodes 1.034
987 Abe Waddington
988 Eddie Leadbeater

989 Don Wilson (42.36)
990 M. Leyland
991 H. Sutcliffe
992 L. Hutton
993 Two
994 G. Boycott and L. Hutton
995 Once
996 Four times
997 C.M. Old
998 H. Verity
999 D.B. Close

LEAGUE CLUBS – 3

1000 Airedale and Wharfedale
1001 York Senior
1002 Huddersfield Central
1003 East Yorkshire Cup
1004 York Senior
1005 South Riding
1006 Yorkshire
1007 South Riding
1008 Huddersfield
1009 East Yorkshire Cup
1010 South Riding
1011 Doncaster
1012 Pontefract
1013 Ribblesdale
1014 Doncaster
1015 Airedale and Wharfedale
1016 Ribblesdale
1017 South Riding
1018 Doncaster
1019 Craven
1020 Central Yorkshire
1021 Pontefract
1022 Humber-Don